15

The Second KIDSTUFF

ITV BOOKS

Published by

Independent Television Books Ltd
247 Tottenham Court Road
London W1P 0AU

In association with Michael Joseph Ltd

First published 1981
© Roger Goffe, 1981

ISBN 0 900727 86 1

Conditions of Sale

Printed by William Clowes (Beccles) Ltd

ALSO AVAILABLE
KIDSTUFF by Roger

The Second KIDSTUFF

By ROGER

ITV BOOKS

in association with

MICHAEL JOSEPH

Instead of all the different cat foods, why don't they make just one that is mouse flavour?

More please! I know my tummy is full but I've room for more in my mouth!

I'm not eating it until the smoke stops!

Why wash my hair? Won't the dirt fall off when you cut it?

I am <u>NOT</u> stupid! its just that I have slow ears!

When I ate six
jellies dad told
me off, but I
think he was
just jealous!

Milk is my
favourite drink
because it
doesn't have
tea leaves at
the bottom!

if there
are rainbows
why aren't there
snowbows?

My dog used
to have
lots of
babies, but
now she's
old, she
just bites
people instead.

My new sister has Dads nose, Mums eyes, and my room!

I don't know what I've done to that ant, but it certainly isn't working!

Mum used to be an actress, but now she's a lady!

Cowboys are very good cattle catchers. They do it with ropes with a moving hole in the end!

I was smacked today for counting my ribs during the biology exam!

When Spot barks and wags his tail, is he angry at one end, and pleased at the other?

In Spring, dogs have puppies, cows have calves, and teachers have tadpoles!

Mum, why did you have a bald baby? Is it 'cos Dad's so old!

When mum took our baby to church, they put him in a bird bath!

How do fishes sit down?

Legs wear down that's why old people are small!

DAddy HIDES his TYPENRITER IN a SeCRET P LAce AWAY FroM BusY LittLe F iNGeRs.

If the sky wasn't there, God would fall through!

I'm slimming Mum, so only one sugar lump in my tea. I'll eat the other ones!

"DEAD" is what happens to you after you've finished up all your birthdays!

I made my Mum a belt for her birthday. I cut it out of Dads leather coat!

If I dont believe in God, would he mind?

It's very lucky the shallow end of the sea is by the beach!

I have four
sisters, and
they're all
girls!

My Daddy is
a plastic surgeon
he mends raincoats

If water had
brakes you
wouldn't need
taps!

Hurray! I can count up to the last number!

My boy friend calls me "slug!"

I love him!

Why does sliced apple go rusty!

I took my knickers off in gym, so no one could peek at them!

It's very expensive, All our family have birthdays in the same year!

Mummy, if by a chance you asked me if I want some sweets, I'd say yes!

Were you ever killed in the war Dad?

When I grow old I want to be a good loud shouter like Mum and Dad!

It's a good
job ink
is cheap,
because I
just spilt
some on
the rug!

Dad, your
clock
stopped
ticking and
died, so I
buried it!

I know where babies come from, but how do all the Mums and Dads get here?

Grandad has lots of lines on his forehead, so he can screw his cap on!

Mum, how do you get so much water in that little tap?

Why do balloons fly in slow motion?

Has anyone ever escaped from school?

Exactly how old is young?

But I don't want a baby brother! I want a TANK!

DYING CAN BE VERY DANGEROUS!

I'm leaving home, as soon as I can reach the door handle!

How do Vet's manage to live? Animals don't have any money!

Besides Jesus, was anyone else born on a holiday?

Our school is very pretty, I do wish I liked it!

... Why am I so unlucky God? I was born on the twenty-third of December, so I was nearly Jesus!

Why didn't you wake me up? You know I can't sleep through thunderstorms but you let me!

I don't think he likes the ones she's got, so Dads bought Mum some shoes with legs on!

First you
tell me to
"use my
  imagination!"
Then you hit
me for lying!

I'm not going
to work when
I grow up!
I'm going to
be a mum
instead!

Mum, when we go in your car, why does everyone toot at us, are we special?

I dont like the city! All the roads are armour plated with cars!

Mum, why does baby sleep all the day, and cry all the night?

why dont shadows have faces ?

I can scream loud enough to give people attacked hearts!

I can talk writing, but I can't read it yet!

Every day I exercise our dog, unless we see a cat, then he exercises me!

Mum, why does your milk always get bigger than the saucepan?

I've hidden your present, so for goodness sake dont go near the wardrobe!

If I'm five today, why am I the same size I was yesterday?

Dad said you're pregnant. If I sit next to you, will I catch it too?

People put
sticky cream
on babies bottoms
to stop their
nappies falling off!

To make a
baby ill you
put it on
your shoulder,
and pat
it's back!

I saw a horse
on fire! When
they took off
the saddle his
back was smoking!

When we go to the pub, Dad always has seconds!

When God made the world, what did he stand on?

Mum, why do I have feet that are bigger than each other?

I have a new
little brother
who eats, and
cries, and sleeps.
I call him
"The Lump!"

I've a hole in
my sock. I've
looked everywhere
for the piece
thats come out
but I can't
find it!

Why do babies always talk scribble?

Scales are the things that tell you the time of your feet!

I have to wear glasses because my eyes are too far apart!

MUM! COME QUICK! THE MILKS BEING SICK ON THE STOVE!

The baby next door is always smoking a dummy!

A signature is a way of writing your name so no one can read it!